Rev. William Fitzgerald

SPEAKING ABOUT DEATH

ACTA PUBLICATIONS

Chicago, Illinois

SPEAKING ABOUT DEATH
Poetic Resources for Ministers of Consolation
by Rev. William J. Fitzgerald

Fr. Fitzgerald is co-pastor of St. Gerald's Parish in Ralston, Nebraska. He is the author of *Beyond Easter* (William C. Brown Publishing, 1990) and the upcoming *Arrow in the Circle* (Ave Maria Press).

**To Father Gerry Weber, my mentor,
. . . with memories of the redwoods—
living poems of eternal life.**

Edited by Gregory F. Augustine Pierce
Artwork and Design by John Dylong
Typography by LINK Book Development and Production

All scripture selections are taken from THE OXFORD ANNOTATED BIBLE, copyright © 1965 by Oxford University Press, Inc., New York, N.Y. The sources for all poetry quotations are contained in the List of References.

Copyright © 1990: ACTA Publications
             4848 N. Clark Street
             Chicago, IL 60640
             312-271-1030

Library of Congress Catalog Number: 89-082384
ISBN: 0-914070-68-1

Printed in the United States of America.

CONTENTS

INTRODUCTION

Even for the person of faith in God and in life hereafter, speaking to others about death—especially at the time of immediate loss and grief—is one of the most difficult assignments. Yet that is what we ministers are regularly asked to do, and we are asked to do it with great sensitivity and insight, often on short notice and for people with whom we are not familiar.

We ministers can view this demand on our time and talent either as a burden to be borne or as an opportunity to be realized and grasped. The challenge for all of us who speak about death is to connect the story of the deceased with the story of grace in a new and effective way.

This book offers some practical suggestions for ministers—ordained or lay—who are asked to speak at death beds, home visits, wake-vigils, funeral services, interments, memorial services or funeral luncheons. It includes poetic reflections to supplement homilies and less formal talks to the grieving in specific death situations. Each of the pages is designed to be removed from the book and inserted into a liturgical rite book, bible, prayer book or homily notes for easy reference. Permission is also granted to reproduce these reflections and to hand them out to the bereaved where appropriate.

I hope that these reflections and poetic resources will be helpful to those who are veterans at the ministry of consolation. It is also meant to be an aid to those who belong to the widening circle of new people called upon to speak publicly at the time of death.

In the future, more deacons, pastoral ministers, and lay men and women will conduct such services. With the increasing mobility of families, multiple marriages, and unaffiliated families, the number of formal wake-vigil services which substitute for church funerals will increase. In addition, the concept of collaborative "team ministry" is especially useful in the ministry of consolation. Rather than having one minister offer all the words of support at the time of death, sharing this responsibility among several people can be both more effective with the mourners and more sensible given the schedules of the ministerial staff.

For example, if a priest or minister is presiding at both a wake-vigil and a funeral service for the same person, it may be especially difficult for him or her to adequately prepare two sets of remarks with fresh insights in each. For this and for various other pastoral reasons—the unavailability of a priest or minister, a special relationship of the deceased with a different member of the pastoral team, and so forth—reflections at the time of death might need to be offered by a variety of persons, lay or clerical.

These then are some reflections on speaking about death from one who has done so many times. I have stood at a loss for words by the caskets of Bill—a great athlete struck down in his prime, of Jimmie—finally home from Vietnam, of Agnes—an innocent victim of a serial murderer. On such occasions we must all—minister and mourner alike—find a passage through the dark. For those of us who believe that Jesus Christ is the light, the darkness holds no final terror. "Wake time" is "vigil time." To keep vigil is to watch for the light.

THE ASSEMBLY OF MOURNERS

A "community of believers" is supposed to gather for the weekly Eucharist. While this ideal is not always met, it is the standard and the goal. At almost every assembly at the time of death, however, the participants are from very diverse backgrounds. Spiritualities vary from deep faith to dormant faith to lack of faith. Participants in the assembly may also come from various denominations or from non-Christian faiths.

This diversity makes it all the more necessary for a minister to consider these questions before speaking to a group:

- Who will be there?
- Where are they "coming from"?
- What do they need?
- What words will reach them?

No matter what the makeup of the assembly of mourners, some common denominators usually apply. They will be at various stages of grief, loss or even anger. Many will sense death as an intruder asserting that we humans are not in complete control of life. Most will need a reason to hope, an alternative to chaos, a strand of meaning, an offering of consolation. Some of these needs must be met before mourners can be moved to "praise God."

The encounter with death is a collision with human limits. Despite all of our technology and medical devices, death intrudes into every life. It seems more like a burglar violating our home rather than an integral stage of human living. Death has a way of jarring us from our mundane pursuits and posing many questions: "Why did this have to happen? What really counts in life? Is this all there is?"

The members of the assembly may be at various stages in facing these questions. Some may even deny the fact of death itself. (There are adults in our country who have never seen a human die; some have never viewed a corpse.)

No matter what their level of faith, those who assemble all swim in a culture which:

- denies the reality of death or cosmeticizes it;
- dulls their senses with an avalanche of images that depict "reality" as new, young, and immortal;
- dispenses a pill to eliminate every pain;
- glorifies winning and sees no redemptive value in loss.

3

In the teeth of our consumer- and pleasure-oriented culture, the church offers one sign—the sign of the cross—at the beginning of life, throughout life, and at the end of life on earth. At death, the assembly of mourners cannot ignore, trivialize or glamorize the cross.

"God" questions abound at death. Those who gather to grieve, no matter what their usual daily thought patterns, do strain to hear the words of everlasting life. They are usually hushed. Their hearts "lean forward." They are ready to hear what they need and want to hear.

THE POETIC WORD

Psychologists would claim that what people need and want to hear at the time of death stems from deep unconscious yearnings common to all people. It is precisely symbol, metaphor, poetry that stretches to meet these deep unconscious yearnings. Poetry is the language of the deep.

Even though the assembly of mourners may be over-dosed by shallow advertising slogans and signs, death opens a window into other symbols of profound meaning. Even though people may be out of touch with these primary symbols, death can provide the opportunity for them to reclaim them.

At the time of death, things like "computer printouts" and "management by objectives" and "logical analysis" fall short. It is then that the poet must speak the language that plumbs the chasm between life and death. The minister of consolation—no matter what his or her own talent or predilection—must provide that poetry.

The minister can find these symbols and metaphors in the Scriptures: "the lilies of the field," "the grain falling into the ground," "the search for a fine pearl." They may also be found in the treasury of human poetic genius.

Will the assembly of mourners be open to the poetic word? Half of the people will be "feeling types." These people are already oriented to the poetic side of life and will respond well to the minister who taps into it. The other half are "thinking types." They are taking time from their computers and their tool boxes to be present. On an ordinary day, these people would probably not even think about opening a book of poetry. However, the day of death is no ordinary day, and even these personality types will be receptive to the poetic word.

Any communication by the minister of consolation must reach the imagination and the heart. It must connect with the unconscious. When such connection occurs, grace will be recognized. When there is no connection, grace may go unobserved.

A WORST CASE SCENARIO

I once substituted for a pastor on vacation when a death occurred. The deceased and the widow and family were totally unknown to me. The man's wife preferred coming to the rectory to make the funeral arrangements. Consequently, the all impor-tant visit to the home was lost, and a whole level of potential understanding and insight was eliminated.

She was a black woman. As the result of our visit, I became aware that her husband had been sick a long time. There was to be only a wake service followed by cremation. We planned the service and she requested that a young friend sing two songs.

When I arrived at the funeral home for the wake-vigil, I discovered that all of the assembly was black, with the exception of myself and one other person. The time came to start and the singer was not there. The funeral director was brusque, suggesting that we "get going." The widow preferred to wait, and so did I. After waiting ten more minutes, however, she signaled for me to begin the service without her friend.

It soon became apparent from the responses that many present were not Catholic. I gave my homily as best I could, reflecting a little on the suffering in this man's life. Halfway through, I thought to myself: "Who am I, this white-Irish-Catholic-priest-stranger speaking about the sufferings of this young black man I have never met?" I was not connecting. My words were touching ears, but not hearts.

Shortly after I finished my remarks, there was a little commotion in the back of the funeral parlor. The young singer had arrived—almost thirty minutes late. (I learned later that she had two small children and her babysitter had not shown up.) The organist was telling her in a stage whisper, "No, there is no way I can play for you. We did not rehearse!"

The young black woman came to the front and mumbled to me, "I guess I won't be able to sing." I asked if she would like to try it without accompaniment. She did. As this woman sang "Precious Lord" *a cappella,* eyes moistened and electricity filled the room. The attention of the assembly of mourners was galvanized. This "minister of consolation" had uttered a "poetic word" in verse and music that was true "soul communication." The single best thing I had done in the entire service was to delay it long enough to allow her time to get there.

There are many lessons to be learned from such experiences. One is that poetry can help the word of God be heard by the heart. Another is that the assembly of mourners can best be reached by a "team effort." (The newly revised Catholic *Order of Christian Funerals* reinforces this insight: "The Church calls each member of Christ's Body—priest, deacon, lay person—to participate in the ministry of consolation.") Finally, the minister of consolation must know and relate to the assembly of mourners in a real and basic way.

That young woman, struggling against great odds just to be present, turned a worst case scenario into a moment of grace.

A BEST CASE SCENARIO

The best ministry of consolation can obviously occur when the pastor and the pastoral team have shared the spiritual journey of the deceased and the assembly of mourners. It was that way with Don. I had seen him many times in his home before he died. It was obvious from pictures in the house, rosaries, and other "clues" that both Don and his wife Martha had a deep devotion to the Blessed Mother.

In his youth and early adulthood, Don had been a sailor. He was an old-timer now, home from the sea. In his last years, he bore the burden of being attached by a plastic cord to a portable oxygen tank. Everywhere he went in the house, it followed. It was like an "albatross" around his neck. After a long battle with emphysema, Don died.

As a part of the funeral homily, I was able to reach into the rich treasury of poetry and utter a poetic word about his death. All of his family and friends who knew about Don's Marian devotion and the plastic cord draped over his shoulder could resonate with the words of Coleridge from *The Rime of the Ancient Mariner:*

> *The self-same moment I could pray;*
> *And from my neck so free*
> *The Albatross fell off, and sank*
> *Like lead into the sea.* *
> *O sleep! it is a gentle thing,*
> *Beloved from pole to pole!*
> *To Mary Queen, the praise be given!*
> *She sent the gentle sleep from Heaven*
> *That slid into my soul.*[1]

I knew from the looks on Don's wife and the rest of the assembly that Mary, Queen of the Sea, as found in the words of the poet Coleridge, was the right word at the right time.

THE UNUSUAL IS THE USUAL

Ministers of consolation have a very challenging task. Every day is different and every death is unique. Perhaps the most difficult death to deal with is that of someone who is a total stranger. We may only know their age, sex and cause of death.

The phone rings. A good parishioner says, "I need a favor. Jerry, a young man in our office was killed last night in a police chase. He was well liked in our office. We don't know the details of the death. They've shipped his body back home for the funeral. My whole office staff is in shock. They are in their twenties, about Jerry's age. We need to do something. I'll let them all off work tomorrow if I could bring them over to the church and you would do some kind of a memorial prayer service. Could you?"

As a pastoral person, you know so well that this "unusual request" is not so unusual at all. What resources can you fall back on in such a situation? You obviously start with the scriptures. Jesus' concern for the young offers fertile ground.

A further resource that can be tremendously helpful in such a situation is to have a file of poetry resources which can be drawn upon quickly. There is a rich vein of poetry that relates to all the human themes. In Jerry's case, the theme is that of the tragic death of a young man. William Shakespeare had something beautiful to say about that:

> . . . when he shall die,
> Take him and cut him out in little stars,
> And he will make the face of heaven so fine
> That all the world will be in love with night.[2]

In Jerry's memorial, the minister of consolation did not use this quote. It was not until he saw how grief stricken the young co-workers were at the loss of their friend that he thought of it.

He did use the gospel story of Peter and John running to the tomb and inserted his own poetic reflection in his short homily:

> One night, Jesus—who was young—could not wait
> for his disciples to arrive.
> He hurried forth from the tomb.
> And now, he is out ahead
> of all the young
> who have hurried forth too soon.
> And he smiles and says to them,
> "Hurry home! Hurry home!"

The young people at the memorial listened intently. Since the majority of them turned out to be unchurched, the poetic verse really did help provide an attention getting window to what the minister had to say. That window helped them look further into the good news about death that only the gospel can bring.

FROM DUST TO DUST—QUICKLY

She was a plucky and dauntless lady. She had survived the dreadful airplane collision at Tenerife, crawling through the flames and dropping to the tarmac below. At age 71, in the burn unit, she waged a valiant battle for survival, and won.

Her death would come 15 years later, due to cancer. This woman had passed through the crucible of fire in life. At death, she did not hesitate to request cremation for her remains. Her request regarding burial was contained in her will and was honored in every detail. There was a Mass of Resurrection with many friends and family members present. The actual burial of the cremated body took place several days later.

On a bitter cold December day, her pastor, nephew, and niece bade last farewell at the grave site. As they told it later: "There was something especially difficult about the burial. It can be a shock to discover the remains of a loved one in a small container, sitting alone next to the grave."

These relatives were face to face with a new and growing practice, the burial of cremated remains apart from the wake and funeral service. This is the beginning of the emergence of an entirely new custom in burial practice. In the years ahead, cremation will become even more widespread than it is today. The economic factor alone will weigh heavily in its favor.

Ministers of consolation must respond to the changing customs surrounding death itself. This poses an additional challenge to speaking about death. Cremation short circuits the natural rhythm of decomposition of the corpse. Like so much else in our "fast lane" society, our bodies are disposed of "instantly." Some funeral directors have noticed an almost callous attitude developing toward the remaining ashes of the dead, with ashes being put in a closet or drawer and forgotten without any burial at all.

Perhaps more than ever, therefore, ministers of consolation will need creative ways to proclaim: "We are more than dust in the wind!" Here again primal images are of great importance. When we used to think of earth as "mother," committal of the body to the ground had an image of planting about it. It held within its very imagery a hint of new life: "Unless the seed of grain fall into the ground. . . ."

Fire, on the other hand, usually connotes destruction and annihilation, even damnation and punishment. Unless we as ministers in some way befriend "Sister Fire" as St. Francis did, it becomes a difficult symbol to deal with at the time of cremation. But it can be done.

Only recently, for example, we have become fully aware that burning is an essential element in the renewing of forests and prairies. If there were never any forest fires, there would be no cleaning out and opening up—followed by renewal and regrowth. And only a year after a prairie fire, wild flowers flourish once again.

In speaking about death, perhaps we must learn to reference the life giving potential of fire if we are to provide meaning to mourners after a cremation. (The Lenten application of ashes, after all, is supposed to be a blessing, not a curse.)

9

SYMBOL SEARCH

The search for the primal symbols, the poetic moods that might speak to the life of any deceased person, is a worthwhile venture. If such symbols can be found, they can greatly enhance words at a deathbed, a wake-vigil reflection, a funeral or memorial service homily, or remarks at an interment.

There are basic universal symbols that are valid everywhere and to every person. The church employs these fundamental cosmic symbols at every death liturgy:

- The casket is met at the doorway (the "narrow gate")—the passage between the elements and the shelter or refuge.
- The Easter or Christ Candle inscribed "Alpha" and "Omega" ("Beginning" and "End") not only images Christ, the Light of the World, but also the primordial Fire that erupted in the beginning of the cosmos.

- Water, which protected us in the womb and created us at baptism, is sprinkled over us again as we are lowered into the ground.

It is of the essence of symbols to help us deal with paradox. Death is the Christian's most pressing paradox: a passage that is an ending and at the same time a beginning. In speaking about death, we must use symbols to attempt to grasp that paradox. In our speech, we reach our limits, but yearn to break through. Poetry helps us leap over our own individual human limits into the mystery that is life-in-death. It gives hints of a "gracious passage," it taps the power of the unconscious, it fans the imagination of new life beyond death.

IMAGINING THE SYMBOLS

One way to get in touch with some of the powerful, primordial symbols of life and death is to bring them into our imagination by way of an imaginary journey. Let your imagination take you away to the desert where you find a meeting tent adorned with paneled tapestries, much like nomadic people have used for centuries. Remove your shoes and enter quietly and reverently.

The first panel that hangs before you is a beautiful tapestry. A golden sun is setting at the left; it begins to sink into the deepest blue sea. As your eye moves to the right, the sea breaks upon the shore. The beach gives way to green trees. In the far corner, the moon begins to rise, and at the right edge—on the horizon—a volcano belches fire and smoke into the edge of the night.

Turning to the right side of the tent, you see another tapestry. It is more simple. Most of it is blue water, but in the center, there is an island. At the very center, there is a tree with outstretched branches. That is all. Look closer. Now you see something not noticed at first. There is a cross just over the top of the tree. Look closer at the island, and you see to one side some sheaves of grain. At the other side, a grape vine bending over from the weight of its purple fruit.

Turning to the left, you observe the last tapestry. It is different again. Its material is black. Embroidered on it are circles in each corner and a larger circle in the middle. Each circle seems to tell a story. The center circle is filled with greenery and naked humans who seem unashamed and many animals. In the upper left circle, an eagle soars into the heavens. In the upper right, a knight in shining armor crosses a narrow bridge over a turbulent river. In the left hand lower circle, a man bandaged from head to toe emerges from a cave, his bonds bursting. In the fifth circle on the right, a gleaming pearl lies on a purple cushion. If you are willing to take the time—to sit in the tent long enough—these images, these icons, these symbols will speak to you in the language of poetry. They will tell you about your own story; they will whisper deep in your psyche.

As you look at the first panel of sun, water, earth, moon, you realize that they are your kin. The elements of your body were with them in the fireball, twelve to twenty billion years ago!

The second tapestry shows the tree of life at the center of the universe. Behind it are the new tree of the cross, surrounded by food for our journey: the bread of life, the wine of gladness.

The third tapestry illustrates primal stories from the dim mists of antiquity: The Flight (or Ascension), the Hero's Quest, the Binding and Loosing, the Pearl of Great Price, and—in the center—the Garden of Paradise.

These archetypal symbols dwell not only "out there," but within each of us. They apply to everyone, they touch all of us. At death, one or another of these symbols may summarize this particular man or that individual woman.

As speakers about death, we need only to look for these signs in the lives of the people about whom we speak.

CLUES TO THE MYSTERY OF A LIFE

The pastoral visit to the home at the time of death can be a great consolation to the family. It can also serve the secondary but important purpose of allowing the minister of consolation to search for clues, symbols or images that fit the unique story of the deceased person.

In this "treasure hunt" the minister is searching for clues of a faith story and the operations of grace. The deceased can no longer speak, but what has been left behind can give hints about the person. Keen attention to clues can help the minister connect the story of the deceased with the story of Jesus.

If there is a yard, notice what it says: is there a garden, flowers, perhaps a shrine? Who gave it loving care? Judge how important all of this is to this unique family.

The doorway is often very symbolic. One homilist made a reference in the funeral homily to Christian hospitality based on the observation of a cheery sign at the front door: "John and Mary Welcome You."

Inside the home, what are the objects and what do they say? Perhaps the environment is plain and simple, even poor and threadbare. What gives it warmth? Where is the main gathering place in this home—the family room, the kitchen?

The montage-type family photo frame with its multiple pictures is a wonderful conversation piece to open into an awareness of this family's story and journey. How long have they lived here? What significant events occurred here?

What objects in the home are hand crafted? What is obviously treasured? Are there awards or trophies? Are there plants and animals?

Are there any symbols that give clues to the family's spirituality? Books? Statues? Pictures?

In every dwelling there is a story. To the degree that the minister of consolation picks up clues from the deceased's home, the family will be more at home with the funeral homily or remarks at the wake-vigil service or interment. In many parishes, the celebrant of the funeral liturgy cannot always make the home visitation. This can be a fruitful opportunity for the exercise of collaborative ministry. Members of the ministerial team can share these clues with each other.

As in all preaching, the task in speaking about death is to move listeners towards the praise of God. This praise is best based on the connection between the personal story of the deceased and the story of salvation. In some situations, the only connection may seem to be the need for God's mercy and the compassion of the Lord. If the minister of consolation searches for clues, however, even more connections with the workings of grace can usually be found.

PREPARING TO SPEAK ABOUT DEATH

What makes preparation for speaking about death so difficult is the crammed time span available. If preparing for regular Sunday homilies is like fixing fine meals, funeral homilies or reflections are like working with pressure cookers. One challenge is how to best use what little time might be available.

One way to maximize that short time is to start the writing process one day and finish it the next. "Sleep on it!" is advice that many business executives are receiving in business seminars. This maxim recognizes the fact that creativity takes place during our dream time. Executives are urged to keep note pads next to their bed stands so they can jot down creative ideas that come to them in their sleep. What applies to executives also applies to ministers of consolation, some of whom firmly believe that they really write their talks in their sleep. Whether it is goals for managers, babies for lovers, or homilies for homilists, creativity does take place in the dark! Even in the compressed time available around funerals, eight hours of quality time can be added to preparation time by starting one's remarks one day and finishing them the next.

Despite the apparent time restrictions surrounding a death, preparation time is not restricted to the period between death and burial. Two thirds of the preparation can be underway long before an actual death occurs. In the preparation for speaking about a person's death, the minister of consolation must telescope his or her attention into three areas: the sacred scriptures, the personal life and prayer experience of the minister, and finally the life experience of the deceased and the family and friends of the deceased. Only the latter must be examined at the eleventh hour.

The prayer life of the minister of consolation and his or her daily interaction with the scriptures is a part of the silence and darkness that gives birth to creativity. Likewise, regular reflection on the primal symbols of life is essential remote preparation for speaking about death.

For the more proximate preparation, in most cases there will be about two days of preparation. Day one is the time for learning as much as possible about the deceased and the assembly of mourners. This begins with a conversation with the funeral director or whoever else notifies the parish about the death. It also includes the pastoral visits to the hospital or home or funeral home.

At the end of the first day, the minister of consolation needs to "cluster" whatever ideas have surfaced. These ideas should be jotted down in clusters or series of words that form associations, words that flow out of your knowledge of the life experience of the deceased or their family.

A pastoral visit, for example, may have revealed that the deceased Martha loved her garden and took many vacations with her husband Mike to the lakes. Thoughts might be clustered this way: "garden-earth-fertility-where was fertility in her life?" or "lakes-fishing-water-the deep, refreshing waters-baptism-new life." The scripture passages which have been chosen can also be a taking-off point for clustering.

After the minister gets down several clusters, one or two will emerge as ideas for a possible theme. Then one or two poems can be found that might fit that particular theme. These poems may not even be used in the minister's actual remarks, but they will help to stimulate the imagination.

When this process is finished, the minister should put it aside and try to get a good night's sleep. There the ideas will work in the unconscious brain for seven or eight hours.

The next day, the theme is put into a rough outline form of the major points to be made. If there is time, this should be left to "simmer" a little longer. Then the homily or remarks should be completed, including any poetic resources which are going to be used.

Many ministers of consolation speak without notes. It helps them maintain direct eye contact with the assembly of mourners. Some use an outline only to help them keep to the point within a definite time frame. Others actually write out their entire remarks.

Many speak directly from the side of the casket. One venerable old Monsignor used to stand with one hand gently on the casket. Perhaps he knew what the communication experts now proclaim: that more than 90% of our communication is non-verbal. We speak about death not only with our tongues but with our faces and our bodies.

No matter where the speaker about death stands or what kind of notes are used, the words spoken can be a work of art guided by the Spirit. When that happens, the imaginations of a grieving assembly become what one minister described as "the dancing partner of faith, the guide into the unknown, the source of creativity."

SOME RECIPES FOR SPEAKING ABOUT DEATH

Good cooks exchange recipes. Perhaps ministers of consolation should do the same.

Most ministers of consolation are so busy performing this essential ministry that they have little time to observe their peers at it. Here is what a few good ministers of consolation say about their own recipes for speaking about death. Their comments are meant to help discover a more poetic approach to the mystery of death.

PRAYER

"I've been speaking about death for 50 years, but I still pray every time to the Holy Spirit, asking 'what would Jesus say in this unique moment?' I then search the scriptures, not just the lectionary, for the appropriate word."

TEAM APPROACH

"As a sister working in pastoral ministry for the last 10 years, I've observed changes in talking about death. Our ministry at the time of death has become more of a team approach and the opportunities for a variety of us to speak has expanded. We help each other out by sharing insights about the deceased with whomever is preparing a talk."

"Wakes are multiplying; priests are decreasing; other pastoral ministers and lay persons are more involved in bereavement ministry. I have often helped families plan wake-vigil services, and this has become much easier with the new *Order of Christian Funerals.*"

"For those who still want the rosary, we recommend the 'Scriptural Rosary' as an option. Each of the mysteries offers an opportunity for mini-reflections. For instance, I recently heard a rosary leader introduce the third glorious mystery this way: 'In this mystery, we recall the disciples, grief stricken, meeting in a closed room together. They were gathered much as we are tonight. They needed the Spirit, the Consoler, and so do we.'"

HOLISTIC APPROACH

"Last year, as a homilist and presider, I had 82 funerals! I rely a lot on the backup of good music and songs that tie into the entire liturgy. A homily should be an integral part of the liturgy, blending with all the other parts."

"In my campus ministry, many people of diverse backgrounds are often present. I take a holistic approach to preaching. Everything should blend together. I make some effort to welcome the strangers and invite them to take part. I am very careful and deliberate and visual with the holy water, the candle, the pall, and the incense. It is body language that connects with the language of the homily."

NO CLICHES

"I avoid giving theological or philosophical answers to the mystery of death. I offer instead hope, support and love. If there are stories to be told, I tell them. I try to relate a story of the deceased to the scripture. I have found the more I theologize, the farther away I am from the listeners. The more I tell stories, the closer I become."

CONNECTING LINK

"As a recently ordained woman minister and being new in the parish, dealing with death is a new challenge. I had to give a reflection upon the death of a grandmother who loved dancing and parties. I searched and searched for some connecting link. I finally thought to add a quote from 'The Lord of the Dance' to my reflection. Many people came up afterward and remarked that they were deeply moved by my connecting the energy of God with the energy of dance. When the right poetic word can be found, it connects with the scriptures in a powerful way."

HUMOR

"Humor sometimes lessens stress. If you know the assembly well, a little gentle humor can be helpful. Only true believers, though, can laugh a little in the face of death."

"I think funerals need the three H's—Healing, Holiness, and Humor. Yes, humor—if used at the right time, at the right place, for the right people."

CREATION SPIRITUALITY

"I find the letting go process of nature, the falling of leaves, the changing of seasons to be good images to help a family enter into grief. I try to move from the 'letting go' to speaking of life, because the message of Jesus is life from death."

ECUMENICAL APPROACH

"As a Catholic pastor, I spent seven years in a rural area that was heavily Lutheran. I found funerals and wakes to be optimum times for ecumenical gestures. I always try to take note of who is in the assembly. I welcome those of other denominations or faiths, make them feel comfortable, invite them to pray. Some of the most positive feedback on my preaching comes from these people."

SIGNS OF THE TIMES

"I served for years as a missionary in Chile and have spent the last twenty years in pastoral work in the U.S.A. I'm very aware of the differences in cultures. As the salesman in *The Music Man* said, 'You've got to know the territory!' Here in the United States the 'territory' is so affluent that a pertinent reflection on death can sometimes contain the reminder: 'Naked I came into this world, and naked, I depart!'"

THE JOURNEY

"The journey symbolism of the scriptures and poetry is helpful. I try to connect the church on earth, the church on the way, and the church arriving. The idea of the communion of saints is very consoling at the time of death."

REPETITION

"Repetition is not always bad. If you have a good insight and it's helpful to people, why not use it with a different assembly? I have a number of outlines that I can pull out at the time of death. As our deaths keep mushrooming, it's very helpful to have a path to follow. Freshness is important though. I've been reviewing my outlines recently and adding some new quotes and even some poetry."

INSPIRING VERSUS EULOGIZING

"I once heard a speaker say, 'Inspiration without expression leads to depression.' I feel a pastoral responsibility to inspire the mourners to praise God the giver of all gifts. I try to communicate in a conversational style, in a way that leads to praise even in the midst of their sorrow. That's difficult. The temptation is to launch into a eulogy in order to lift their spirits. I try to avoid that because I do not believe that preaching the word is about eulogizing an individual person or life. You can still say some good things about the deceased without making your remarks into a eulogy."

A BLESSING STRUCTURE

"I often use a litany formula at the very end of my remarks, after completing my reflection on the scripture and its relation to the life of the deceased. I've found that no matter whom I have buried, I've always been able to find something for which to praise God. I try to pick out a few pertinent facts in the life of the deceased that can be put in a prayer of praise and thanksgiving. Here is an example:

And so we come to Eucharist always to praise God for good gifts. In the life of John, we praise God for these gifts given to him:

- the blessing of his forty-five years of marriage with Sarah;
- the blessing of his three children and seven grand-children;
- the blessing of water, which so refreshed John in his love of fishing and which first gave him the promise of new life through the sacrament of Baptism.

For all these gifts, and for many more, we praise God!"

POETIC REFLECTIONS
FOR SPECIFIC SITUATIONS

Look steadily at the darkness.
It won't be long before you see the light.
                            Anthony de Mello, S.J.[3]

The following poetic reflections are divided by age or state in life, type of death, and special affinities.

Each reflection might suffice as a short talk in itself or be inserted into a homily or a fuller set of remarks.

Since these reflections are written to be given orally, it is important that the speaker spend some preparation time practicing them aloud. They should be delivered in a cadence which is deliberate and more dramatic than that used in a prose reading. Commas, ellipses, dashes should elicit distinct pauses. It is recommended that key words or phrases be underlined or highlighted during the preparation. In those places where a name is to be inserted, a proper pronoun chosen or an appropriate choice made based on the individual situation, this should be done beforehand and clearly marked to avoid confusion or embarrassment.

STILLBORN

I am the good shepherd; I know my own and my own know me.

John 10:14

And Jesus is our true Mother
in whom we are endlessly carried
and out of whom
we will never come.

Julian of Norwich[4]

We want our lives to count.
So what of this life stillborn?

If to count means to call forth love,
to elicit compassion, to be missed,
then by all earthly reckoning,
this child counts!

But there is another measure.
One that mocks our computations.

The Good Shepherd counts his sheep,
and the old ones flock through his gate;
but only the little ones, the lambs,
are carried in his arms.

23

INFANT

ave you never read, "Out of the mouth of babes and sucklings thou hast brought perfect praise"?

Matthew 21:16

O she doth teach the torches to burn bright!
It seems she hangs upon the cheek of night
Like a rich jewel in an Ethiop's ear—
Beauty too rich for use, for earth too dear!

William Shakespeare, *Romeo and Juliet*[5]

Such can be said of this dear child,
taken like a precious jewel,
a holy innocent,
from his/her parents' house.

25

> We pray not for him/her;
> he/she is with the Lord.
> We pray for us,
> that the Lord be with us.

When sudden death comes
like a thief in the night,
we are left with anger and fear,
numbness and groping.

> Like the first Christmas families,
> mourning the innocents,
> so beautiful the gift,
> so great the loss.

(continue)

May those Holy Innocents,
And the kids who led the Lord
on the Sunday of Palms,
welcome little _____ (name).

> May his/her beauty "too rich for use
> and for earth too dear"
> be this family's beacon
> beyond their tears.

Let him/her "teach torches to burn bright"
as he/she effortlessly passes through,
and patiently awaits our coming
through the narrow gate.

TODDLER

 **R**ound the throne was a rainbow that looked like an emerald.

Revelation 4:3

Three years she grew in sun and shower,
Then Nature said, "A lovelier flower
On earth was never sown;
This Child I to myself will take;
She shall be mine, and I will make
A Lady of my own."

William Wordsworth, "Three Years She Grew"[6]

Is heaven like an exclusive suburban enclave,
"No old folks or little children allowed here!"

Is heaven a paved over, bricked-in
complex of row houses,
marked, "exclusive occupancy"?

Is heaven a tower in the sky,
soaring so far above the song of birds
and the chatter of children?

Could heaven be bliss without children?
Is not our terrible loss,
Heaven's great gain?

YOUNG CHILD

**A**nd they were bringing children to him, that he might touch them; and the disciples rebuked them. But when Jesus saw it, he was indignant, and said to them, "Let the children come to me, do not hinder them, for to such belongs the kingdom of God.

Mark 10:13–14

Ah cruel tree! If I were you
and children climbed me, for their sake
though it be winter, I would break
into spring blossoms—white and blue.

Oscar Wilde, "Le Jardin Des Tuileries"[7]

The aspen leaves flutter in the breeze,
like a million angel wings.
There is a legend that they have trembled
  for 2000 years,
ever since a sturdy trunk was felled
  and fashioned into a cross.

    Or, are they more like gold robed monks
      exclaiming: Holy, Holy, Holy.
    Innocence has been nailed to our arms,
    But we have borne him to Easter glory!

Aspens are the children of the forest,
first to resurrect from the ashes of summer fires.
Dancing in the wind, they will await the elder conifers
whose life is longer.

(continue)

Splashed above the ashes of summer's fire,
from golden splendor, they rustle and proclaim:
All children shall be first
to rise again!

PRE-TEEN

hen children were brought to him that he might lay his hands on them and pray. The disciples rebuked the people; but Jesus said, "Let the children come to me, and do not hinder them; for to such belongs the kingdom of heaven." And he laid his hands on them and went away.

Matthew 19:13–15

Then come home, my children, the sun is gone down,
And the dews of the night arise;
Come, come, leave off play, and let us away
Till the morning appears in the skies.

William Blake, "Nurse's Song"[8]

On our earthly journey,
adults lead children out of play
into work.

On our heavenly journey,
might children lead adults out of work
into play?

If we only value work,
then a child's loss is total loss.

But if playful openness to life is of great value,
are not children at home in heaven?

When the Kingdom comes,
will we be led in by skipping and laughing children?

YOUNG BOY

 am the Alpha and the Omega," says the Lord God, who is and who was and who is to come, the Almighty.

Revelation 1:8

A boy's will is the wind's will,
And the thoughts of youth are long, long thoughts.

William W. Longfellow, "My Lost Youth"[9]

He is the Alpha-Omega, Lord of the universe,
  the Incarnate Word,
and yet he cannot remember old age, for it never came!
He cannot recall mid-life, for it was cut short—
the cross thrust between youth and fullness of life.

> The death of the young is hardest to bear;
> the cross intersects earthly hopes and dreams
> and the thoughts of youth
> that are "long, long thoughts."

But we entrust _____ (name) to Jesus,
  who once was _____ (age)
and ran with the wind.
The Lord does remember _____ (age)
  with all its dreams,
and knows there is more
  beyond our faint imaginings.

(continue)

"A boy's will is the wind's will,
And the thoughts of youth are long, long thoughts."
The hero's quest, the search for the pearl,
the contest, the challenge, the victor's thrill.

> Like a superb athlete,
> _____ (name) has vaulted over
> the hurdles of adulthood,
> surpassing what we could ever dream.

There, beyond, may he run with Jesus,
and grasp the prize towards which we slowly strive.

YOUNG GIRL

 ut Jesus called them to him, saying, "Let the children come to me, and do not hinder them; for to such belongs the kingdom of God."

Luke 18:16

The knowingness of little girls
Is hidden underneath their curls.

Phyllis McGinley, "What Every Woman Knows"[10]

The "knowingness of little girls"
dwells in the wonder years
of "OOHS" and "AHS."

    The "knowingness of little girls"
    is not tasting bitter fruit,
    nor deep regret.

The "knowingness of little girls"
knows "Dad" and "Mom"—
and "God"—as love.

    May our many tears and years
    not blind our own knowingness
    that _____ (name) waits for us.

TEENAGE BOY

hey both ran, but the other disciple outran Peter and reached the tomb first; and stooping to look in, he saw the linen cloths lying there.

John 20:4-5

The winds of God's grace are always blowing,
but we must make an effort to lift our sails.

Vincent Dwyer[11]

The young boy cannot wait for second—
he steals belly down.

> The young sail with the wind,
> pushing the limits with zest.

The "exuberance of youth,"
Would we have it otherwise?

> And yet, there is a danger line
> between sliding safe
> and being out.

Some die in the exuberance of youth.

> One night, Jesus—who was young—could not wait
> for his disciples to arrive.
> He hurried forth from the tomb.
> And now, he is out ahead
> of all the young
> who have hurried forth too soon.

And he smiles and says to them:
"Hurry home! Hurry home!"

TEENAGE GIRL

he bridegroom came, and those who were ready went in with him to the marriage feast.

Matthew 25:10

Say that upon the altar of her beauty
You sacrifice your tears, your sighs, your heart.
Write till your ink be dry, and with your tears
Moist it again, and frame some feeling line
That may discover such integrity. . .

William Shakespeare, *The Two Gentlemen from Verona*[12]

Teenage is a poem being written
a lyric to be sung.
No other time is so specially named
as the "teenage years."

39

It is that transit time
from pinafore to promenade,
that time to know who we are,
and who we might become.

_____ (name) knew, as much as we,
her true identity:
cherished daughter, (sister), friend, classmate,
sister of Jesus, confidante of Mary, child of God.

She knew too the gospel story
of the maidens
—the wise and the foolish—
awaiting the bridegroom's return.

(continue)

Her vessel was filled
with the holy oils of baptism and confirmation.
Her lamp was burning brightly
when He came.

40

YOUNG MAN

**A**nd we have the prophetic word made more sure. You will do well to pay attention to this as to a lamp shining in a dark place, until the day dawns and the morning star rises in your hearts.

2 Peter 1:19

. . . when he shall die,
Take him and cut him out in little stars,
And he will make the face of heaven so fine
That all the world will be in love with night.

William Shakespeare, *Romeo and Juliet*[13]

One star hangs in the heavens;
another streaks across the sky,
a blaze of beauty.

    Who can say which is greater—
    the steady long lived glimmer,
    or the shooting star?

    _____'s (name's) destiny is Christ's light,
so in your dark place
gaze towards the east
"as to a lamp shining"
until the first streaks of dawn appear
and the morning star rises in your hearts.

YOUNG WOMAN

 esus said to her, "Mary." She turned and said to him in Hebrew, "Rabboni!" (which means Teacher). Jesus said to her, "Do not hold me, for I have not yet ascended to the Father; but go to my brethren. . . ."

John 20:16–17

Shall I compare thee to a summer's day?
Thou art more lovely and more temperate.
Rough winds do shake the darling buds of May,
And summer's lease hath all too short a date. . . .

But thy eternal summer shall not fade,
Nor lose possession of that fair thou ow'st;
Nor shall Death brag thou wander'st in his shade,
When in eternal lines to time thou grow'st.
So long as men can breathe, or eyes can see,
So long lives this, and this gives life to thee.

William Shakespeare, Sonnet XVIII[14]

43

We commend _____ (name) to that company
whose "summer shall not fade":
to Mary, messenger of Easter joy,
to Lucy, bearer of light,
to Cecilia, Kateri, and Teresa of the Little Flower,
short lived all, but long remembered.

(continue)

May that youthful company take
_____ (name) to the banquet hall of heaven,
where "Rabboni,"
now ascended to the Father,
will embrace her,
and speak her name among the saints.

44

ADULT

I will give you the keys of the kingdom of heaven, and whatever you bind on earth shall be bound in heaven, and whatever you loose on earth shall be loosed in heaven.

Matthew 16:19

But he brought a lifetime of prayer to death's door;
and in a little while, it entered there with him.

Paul Horgan[15]

In adolescence—the keys to the car,
our world grew wider.
In adulthood—the keys to a home,
our world grew warmer.
At work—the keys to safe and ledger,
our world grew heavier.

But the keys to the Kingdom are light
and they are worn thin from
unlocking hearts with kindness,
unlocking creativity with praise,
unlocking hope with a smile.

_____ (name) has been given the keys of the kingdom.
May they fit easily in Peter's gate,
and give entry to life everlasting.

ADULT CO-WORKER

**W**hen evening came, his disciples went down to the sea, got into a boat, and started across the sea to Capernaum. It was now dark, and Jesus had not yet come to them.

John 6:16–17

One has seen, in such steadiness never deflected,
how by darkness a star is perfected.

Marianne Moore, "By Disposition of Angels"[16]

Between ending evening hours of five and six
shadow fingers lay their prints
upon the valleys and hills
and softly nudge concrete walls.
Pigeons flutter, commuters huddle,
word processors wind down.
The Dow is closed.
The door is locked.
Day is done.

47

So too in the evening years of fifties and sixties,
light and shadow merge
the mellow times, the vintage years—
satisfaction comes to terms with life.
And even when death's darkness intervenes,
the evening star promises tomorrow.
Christ has died;
Christ is risen;
Christ will come.

(continue)

In the steadiness of a friend's life,
the star is always present.
It is only in the dark
that it takes its rightful place.

48

WIFE OR SWEETHEART

In those days, Mary arose and went with haste into the hill country, to a city of Judah, and she entered the house of Zechariah and greeted Elizabeth.

Luke 1:39–40

I love thee with a love I seemed to lose
With my lost saints—I love thee with the breadth,
Smiles, tears, of all my life!—and, if God choose,
I shall love thee better after death.

Elizabeth Barrett Browning, *Sonnets from the Portuguese*[17]

**It has been; it shall be,
women have a story to unfold.
Ever since a maiden hastened
through the hills
to tell Elizabeth.**

49

**At Cana and Samaria's well,
women in the Jesus story
witnessed to their friends
of vintage wine
and holy water.**

**And at Easter's early dawning,
women first to the tomb,
expecting death, meeting life,
were first to believe
the saving story.**

(continue)

It has been so with _____ (name).
She has a tale she could not wait to tell
of the sweetness of life
and verse upon verse
of love and caring.

50

HUSBAND OR SWEETHEART

hen Simon Peter heard that it was the Lord, he put on his clothes, for he was stripped for work, and sprang into the sea.

John 21:7

There is an energy in us
which makes things happen
when the paths of other persons
touch ours. . . .

Monks of the Weston Priory, "Wherever You Go"[18]

We recall today
the paths of male energy,
even unto the cross.

51

Wild geese on the wing
hunters hunkering down,
wingbacks sweeping wide.

The beat of the drum
the cadence call,
sunrise, reveille.

The pursuit of work,
romancing a mate/sweetheart
taking risks to grow.

Lifting up a child,
shouldering heavy tasks,
standing by a friend.

(continue)

Encountering the limits,
steadfast in suffering,
never losing heart.

The male energy
surging forth with the Lord,
one last run home.

52

PARENT

**B**ut they who wait for the Lord
shall renew their strength,
they shall mount up with wings
like eagles,
they shall run and not be weary,
they shall walk and not faint.

Isaiah 40:31

The eagle . . . lays its eggs only once a year in a
place so inaccessible that there is room only for the
nest. The nest is exposed to freezing cold and high
winds, yet in this perilous place, the eagle lays down
its most precious gift. Our prayers should be like the
flight of eagles. They will be sent skyward on eagle
wings to touch the ear of God.

Carl Hammerschlaug, M.D.[19]

53

**The eagle's flight, like human parenting,
gives shelter, food, and faith,
in rough terrain.**

> **Watching the brood with eagle eye,
> making the daily commute,
> coming home, always faithful.**

**Pulled towards earth,
by turbulence,
yet circling towards the sun.**

(continue)

Soaring with joy when eaglets learn to fly.
And when strength is gone,
flying beyond the rim,
towards the morning star.

54

ELDERLY

hen I was a child, I spoke like a child, I thought like a child, I reasoned like a child; when I became a man, I gave up childish ways. For now we see in a mirror dimly, but then face to face. Now I know in part; then I shall understand fully, even as I have been fully understood.

1 Corinthians 13:11-12

Take kindly the counsel of the years,
gracefully surrendering the things of youth.
Nurture strength of spirit
to shield you in sudden misfortune.

The Desiderata[20]

We go
from letting be,
to letting go,
to letting God—
take what is left.

> Youth ascends,
> pushes forward,
> generates,
> rushes on,
> only to surrender
> to mid-life.

The middle years consolidate,
re-appraise,
mellow,
and stretch
toward the golden years.

(continue)

Hearing fails,
touch trembles,
sight dims,
senses give way
to insightful,
grace-filled wisdom.

> In letting go
> of the periphery,
> we are drawn
> to the center
> and vortexed
> into the heartbeat
> of the universe.

ADDICTION

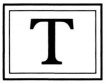

T o the weak I became weak, that I might win the weak.

1 Corinthians 9:22

For all that has been—Thanks!
For all that shall be—Yes!

Dag Hammerskjöld[21]

To finally say "yes" to death
Can be to say "yes" to life.
"For your faithful, Lord,
life is changed, not ended."

> To say "yes" to life
> is to say "yes"
> to growing and changing,
> to taking hold,
> and to letting go.

To say "yes" to life
is to rejoice
in the half filled vessel,
and not complain
for what was lost.

> To say "yes" to life
> is to acknowledge
> a supreme power,
> and to live
> one day at a time.

(continue)

To be emptied, but still filled,
to be tied down, yet set free,
is to discover the prize,
the key to locked up life.

58

AIDS

lothe yourselves, all of you, with humility toward one another, for "God opposes the proud, but gives grace to the humble."

1 Peter 5:5

What began as a modest remembrance of a few who succumbed to AIDS has become one of the nation's most moving memories—a quilt the size of nearly eight football fields, containing over eight thousand panels, three feet by six feet. Produced by friends and relatives, each commemorates a single life lost to AIDS.

Time, October 10, 1988[22]

59

Is our journey towards the Kingdom of God
like the making of a quilt,
piecing the patches together as we go?

> There is no perfect quilt,
> no seamless cloak.
> The lives of all of us are patchy.

Each fabric is unique,
different from the rest,
and no one has it sewn completely together.

> For some, the last cloth in the quilt
> is the patch of suffering,
> and their badge of courage.

(continue)

The ugly patch called AIDS,
when turned over by love,
is the color of hope.

Now folded in faith,
may the pattern of _____'s (name's) death
reveal new life to those of us who still sew.

ALZHEIMER'S

 consider the sufferings of this present time are not worth comparing with the glory that is to be revealed to us. . . . the creation itself will be set free from its bondage to decay and obtain the glorious liberty of the children of God.

Romans 8:18,21

Judge not the Lord by feeble sense,
But trust Him for His grace;
Behind a frowning providence,
He hides a smiling face.

William Cowper, "Light Shining Out of Darkness"[23]

Smiles and happy faces are the stuff
of nice days and yellow stickers.

61

    In the senior care centers dotting our land,
    there are smiles, but also frowns.

There are furrowed brows, and
tear stained cheeks, and vacant stares.

    Alzheimer's steals in like the fog,
    obscuring, confusing, beclouding.

For many, it is the final tracing of the cross
on memory, thought, and sense.

    Alzheimer's is a sepulcher, a resting place,
    but no less holy than the happy places.

Beneath the stony unknowing,
the Spirit of God still hovers.

(continue)

Dwelling deep in each heart,
ready to enliven us beyond unknowing.

>"Lift up your hearts!"
>"We have lifted them up to the Lord."

May the Spirit now lift up
what was deepest in _____'s (name's) heart.

>So that what "was seen dimly, as in a mirror,"
>he/she shall now "understand fully."

CANCER

 have fought the good fight, I have finished the race, I have kept the faith. Henceforth there is laid up for me a crown of righteousness. . . .

2 Timothy 4:7–8

In Flanders fields the poppies blow
Between the crosses, row on row,
That mark our place; and in the sky
The larks, still bravely singing, fly. . . .

John McCrae, "In Flanders Fields"[24]

Flanders and Iwo's sands
mark wars waged in other lands.
Yet not all battles are removed,
some are very close at hand.

Cancer, the malignant foe,
battles within our gates.
And we marshal fortitude,
and the best of human traits.

Facing endurance and chemo,
its legions sound retreat.
Only to attack again,
and the body seem to beat.

And then there comes a deathly peace
until within the still
life's captain stirs and behold,
release comes o'er the hill.

63

(continue)

And those who lost brave battles,
will rise to win the war,
and death itself be vanquished,
and tears shall be no more.

       _____ (name), we commend you to the captain,
you have fought the bitter fight,
now freed from pain and suffering,
may you rejoice forever in the light.

GREAT PAIN

**I** am not at ease, nor am I quiet; I have no rest;
but trouble comes.

Job 3:26

If like Job we ask "Why must I suffer?"
we will give vast amounts of energy
to an unanswerable question.

If instead we ask "How am I suffering?"
we will enter into a sacred journey
where God's love will be found in the new life.

Paula Ripple[25]

Pain is comfort's absence, a dreadful no-thing.
The pain of dying empties life as we know it.
For those who mourn,
 this depletion fills our cup with tears,
but is a chalice held with tender trembling.

> Courting, marrying, loving is a filling up
> and a bursting of passion.
> Suffering, waiting, and dying seem emptying,
> but are the very filling up of the cup of
> compassion.

Our departed loved one might say to you:
"Never were you so tender, never so compassionate,
as when we shared that cup.
And now we have shared fully the cup of Jesus,
and we shall not drink it again
 until the kingdom of God."

HEART ATTACK

or where your treasure is, there will your heart be also.

Luke 12:34

Our hearts are restless
until they rest in thee.

St. Augustine[26]

We recall the heart beats of a lifetime,
cut short by sudden death:
a heart that did a lifetime of work,
a heart that loved _____ (names of family or friends),
a heart that beat with compassion,
a heart that wore out from loving, and living,
and serving.

67

In this sudden loss, our own hearts
are numbed with dismay,
and so we ask that:
the love of Christ
will be poured into our hearts,
the love we feel for _____ (name)
will warm and console us,
the love we feel for each other
will grow,
the love of _____ (name) for us
will live on in our memories.

(continue)

"Our hearts are restless
until they rest with thee!"
May _____'s (name's) heart
finally be at peace with thee.
This we ask
through Christ our Lord.

NATURAL DISASTER

**D**o you not know that all of us who have been baptized into Christ Jesus were baptized into his death? We were buried therefore with him by Baptism into death, so that as Christ was raised from the dead by the glory of the Father, we too might walk in newness of life.

Romans 6:3–4

Be praised my Lord by lowly Sister Water. . .
making us young again in baptism and in rain.

"Canticle of St. Francis"[27]

Fire, air, water, earth:
we cannot live without them.

69

They nurture, warm, cleanse us.
They are our life companions.

So when the sources of life bring death,
our shock is all the greater.

And yet, they themselves in their own journeys,
have to die.

Wells run dry, the fire ebbs,
the earth is mantled with snow.

But they spring up again:
sparks, budding earth, the gentle rains.

If they are to die and rise,
is our glory any less?

(continue)

There is a fountain of youth,
it is the font of baptism.

May its overflowing promise life,
not death.

SERIOUS ILLNESS

Let us run with perseverance the race that is set before us, looking to Jesus the pioneer and perfecter of our faith, who for the joy that was set before him endured the cross, despising the shame, and is seated at the right hand of the throne of God.

Hebrews 12:1–2

Angels, beautiful pauses in the whirlwind,
Be with us through the seasons of unease. . . .

May Sarton, "The Beautiful Pauses"[28]

1984—Los Angeles—Joan Benoit,
running for the gold,
is every woman or man
bravely running
the marathon of pain.

> Through city streets,
> past blurring crowds,
> people reaching out
> but still,
> she must run alone.

Twists, turns, straightaways
and then the tunnel,
that dark passage
into the heart
of the city of the Angels.

(continue)

71

Enduring pain, pushing on,
letting go of sunlight
and the road of life—
plunging into the tunnel
and toward the light.

Then bursting into a hundred thousand
welcomes,
glorious light—
the torch burning brightly,
the last lap to glory.

Having run the race and stayed the course,
_____ (name),
may the martyrs and saints
come to cheer you
into the City of the Angels!

STROKE OR LIFE SUPPORT SYSTEM

T ruly, truly, I say to you, when you were young, you girded yourself and walked where you would; but when you are old, you will stretch out your hands, and another will gird you and carry you where you do not wish to go.

John 21:18

That self-same moment I could pray;
And from my neck so free
The Albatross fell off, and sank
Like lead into the sea.

Samuel Taylor Coleridge, *The Rime of the Ancient Mariner*[29]

Monitors, tubes, machines are
our modern way of saying
life is precious,
support life!

> Yet there comes a point in time
> on the way to new life,
> when they become bonds
> that restrain.

They are cast away now
like the Albatross, and
_____ (name) is set free
for new life.

> With the ancient mariner,
> and St. Peter the fisherman,
> we praise the Lord,
> for freedom.

SUFFERING

or the word of the cross is folly to those who are perishing, but to us who are being saved it is the power of God.

1 Corinthians 1:18

. . . we are to sink eternally
from letting go
to letting go into God.

Meister Eckhart[30]

I asked God for strength that I might achieve;
I was made weak that I might learn humbly to obey.

I asked for health that I might do greater things;
I was given infirmity that I might do better things.

I asked for all things that I might enjoy life;
I was given life that I might enjoy all things.

I got nothing I asked for, but everything I
hoped for;
Almost despite myself, my unspoken prayers
were answered.

I am—among all men—most richly blessed.

(Written by an anonymous Confederate soldier)

SUICIDE

A nd a storm of wind came down on the lake, and they were filling with water, and were in danger. And they went and woke him, saying, "Master, Master, we are perishing! And he awoke and rebuked the wind and the raging waves."

Luke 8:23–24

. . . I am rowing, I am rowing
though the oarlocks stick and are rusty
and the sea blinks and rolls
like a worried eyeball,
but I am rowing, I am rowing,
though the wind pushes me back. . . .

Anne Sexton, "Rowing"[31]

We gather in a vale of tears,
beneath a cloud of uncertainty.
"Whys" and "if onlys"
give us no rest.

Yet in our searching we find certitude:
the ending of _____'s (name's) life
was not right for him/her,
and was not right for us.

When our boat seems so small,
the waves so large,
we must find a better port
than this.

(continue)

For _____ (name),
the enemy Death poured through.
But it is not for us to judge
defenses that did not hold.

> And what of God?
> Our Creator is surely strong enough
> to pick up the pieces
> of self-ended lives.

Will our God who marks the sparrow's course
judge life by one moment of ending
or by the rowings of a lifetime
toward the shore?

TRAVEL ACCIDENT

 **T**hen they told what had happened on the road, and how he was known to them in the breaking of the bread.

Luke 24:35

The good road and the road of difficulties
you have made to cross,
and where they cross
that place is holy.

Black Elk[32]

So often the road we travel
is towards a gracious arrival:
to school, to work, to a holiday,
and—best of all—home again.

> The highways, avenues, streets
> are but friendly markers
> between going and coming,
> arriving and departing.

Then chaos intervenes.
"Cross-Roads" take new meaning,
our paths intersect and crash
and are splintered in the cross.

> Our path is now the Via Dolorosa—
> the road of sadness,
> the path of sorrow,
> the Way of the Cross.

(continue)

It takes us to the Mount of Olives,
and to Calvary and the tomb beyond,
but it also stretches to Emmaus
And on towards Easter glory.

    May _____ (name), who is now on that
     Emmaus Road,
    find peace and lodging and rest,
    for the day is now far spent,
    and his/her journey is done.

LOVER OF NATURE

ike a tree planted by streams of water, that yields its fruit in its season, and its leaf does not wither.

Psalm 1:3

I see his blood upon the rose
And in the stars, the glory of his eyes. . . .
His cross is every tree.

Joseph Mary Plunkett, "I See His Blood upon the Rose"[33]

For hands that have turned the black earth,
Ears that have heard the cry of the dove,
Eyes that have seen daffodils through the snow,
A heart that has beat to the rhythm of spring—
Winter's death is but Christ's white burial shroud,
cast aside when the skylark sings to the morning star,
And the sun's first rays burst open tulips . . .
and someday tombs.

81

LOVER OF THE SEA, LAKES, RIVERS

ollow me and I will make you become fishers of men.

Mark 1:17

The seed is with Christ
  and the harvest is with Christ.
May we be gathered into God's granary.

The sea is with Christ and the fish are with Christ.
May we be swept into God's nets.

From growth to maturity,
  and from maturity to death,
May you, O Christ,
  close your arms tightly around us!

From death to finish—oh, it is not finish,
  but a new growth.
May we be found dwelling
  in the paradise of the graced!

Traditional Gaelic poem[34]

83

**We are carried,
we are swept,
we are found,
we are graced!**

> **The Lord of the sea,
> From spring to fall,
> His is the spawning,
> and we are the catch.**

**From our weight
His net will never break.**

PERSON CREMATED

**F**or he knows our frame;
he remembers that we are dust.

Psalm 103:14

music you loved has filled like autumn with sadness
and places we used to be I can hardly bear
flowers are less than flowers days are of—darkness
something fell like a leaf when you went away

Desmond Egan, "Requiem"[35]

Are we no more than falling leaves,
or "dust in the wind"?

> **Is Ash Wednesday's smudge a cruel curse,**
> **or a surprising blessing?**

Surely God who shaped the sun and moon from dust
can do as much for us?

> **Each speck in the universe was there**
> **in the fire-ball, at the beginning.**

Is it too much to expect that every life
will be reshaped in the ending?

> **We are sparks from God's anvil,**
> **and our Easter fire shapes us anew.**

Christ, Lord of fire and earth and water,
May these ashes rest till your Spirit
  whirls them into life.

PERSON WITH DISABILITY

**A**nd when Jesus came to the place, he looked up and said to him, "Zachaeus, make haste and come down; for I must stay at your house today."

Luke 19:5

"Broken things are powerful."
Things about to break are stronger still.
The last shot from the brittle bow is truest.

Eugene McCarthy, "Courage at Sixty"[36]

Long ago, a branch about to break
raised short Zachaeus
high above the crowd
to meet the Lord.

> There once was a soldier, Ignatius,
> with a wounded leg
> but a heart so large
> he enlisted with the Lord.

Kateri, Lily of the Mohawks,
was an orphaned child
whose half blind eyes
clearly saw the Lord.

> Disabilities and the cross of Christ
> are hewn from the same wood.
> To be disabled
> is to know the disabled Lord.

RECOVERED ALCOHOLIC

 et each of you look not only to his own interests, but also to the interests of others. Have this mind among yourselves, which you have in Christ Jesus.

Philippians 2:4–5

God grant us the serenity
to accept the things we cannot change,
courage to change the things we can,
and the wisdom to know the difference.

Serenity Prayer[37]

The first tiny, teetering steps of baby
were acknowledged and applauded with glee.

89

Then came the tentative steps
out of the cocoon,
towards kindergarten
and the larger world.

(If applicable):
There were the cadenced military steps,
drilled and honed, precise and in order.

(If applicable):
In adulthood, those measured, solemn steps
to the altar—two paths merging into one.

And there were the faltering steps of illness,
turned away from destruction by twelve better steps.

(continue)

Those were the steps towards redemption,
the path of conversion, the grace filled steps!

> For all the steps of _____'s (name's) life,
> we praise God,
> and for the footprints of Jesus beside him,
> we give thanks.

SYMBOL REFLECTIONS

*The Miracles of the Church seem to me to rest not so much
upon faces or voices or healing power coming suddenly near
us from afar off, but upon our perceptions being made finer,
so that for a moment our eyes can see and our ears can hear
what is there about us always.*

Willa Cather, *Death Comes to the Archbishop*[38]

Symbols are what the Church uses to help us "see and
hear what is about us always." They can open the door to the
mystery of life in death. Those who have been apart from the
symbols of the Church will perhaps have their "perceptions
made finer" by the death of a loved one. Much benefit can come
from their encounter with old, familiar symbols.

These symbol reflections might be used within a wake-
vigil, at a funeral homily, or at some other moment during the
ministry of consolation. They can be links in re-connecting
mourners with some of the rich liturgical symbols the Church
uses to speak about death.

BIBLE

 lso another book was opened, which is the book of life.

Revelation 20:12

Now at last, they were beginning Chapter One
of the Great Story,
which no one on earth has read,
which goes on forever,
in which every chapter
is better than the one before.

C. S. Lewis[39]

**This Holy Book is our book;
Its story is our story.**

> **We are Zachaeus, too short,
> yet called to the banquet.**

**We are Mary of Magdala, sinful,
but loving much.**

> **We are Levi, doing our business,
> and our Lord is there.**

**We are Martha, very busy,
and our Lord is there too.**

> **We are Lazarus, who died,
> and for whom Jesus wept.**

**We are _____ (family members), saddened,
yet continuing the story "which goes on forever."**

(continue)

Praise God for the Scripture stories!
Praise God for our story!
Praise God for gracious endings . . .
which are but beginnings.

Amen!

BREAD

 **I** am the living bread which came down from heaven; if anyone eats of this bread, he will live forever; and the bread which I shall give for the life of the world is my flesh.

John 6:51

A handful of wheat, five thousand years old,
was found in the tomb
of one of the kings
of ancient Egypt.
Someone planted the grains
and, to the amazement of all,
the grains came to life.

Anthony de Mello, S.J.[40]

95

For many years,
the grains of Eucharistic wheat
have been planted in the soul of _____ (name).

We commend that wheat
to the Lord of the harvest.
May it grow into everlasting life.

CANDLE

e is the beginning, the first-born from the dead, that in everything he might be pre-eminent.

Colossians 1:18

I have seen too many stars
to let the darkness
overwhelm me.

Macrina Wiederkehr, OSB[41]

Our Christ candle is no brief flickering,
it is our pillar of fire in the night.

Inscribed Alpha, the beginning,
and Omega, the end point,
it lights the chasm between death and life.

The blessed incense grains embedded in His wounds
signify Christ's offering—a pleasant fragrance.

May the love and service of _____'s (name's) life
be imbedded in our memories
like incense in this wax.

And may this candle light his/her way on the journey,
and be our consolation on this dark night.

CHALICE

nd he took a cup, and when he had given thanks he said, "Take this, and divide it among yourselves; for I tell you that from now on I shall not drink of the fruit of the vine until the kingdom of God comes.

Luke 22:17–18

Then they went to Sir Galahad,
where he still knelt in prayer,
and behold he was dead;
for what he had been praying for had happened:
in the moment when he had seen the vision,
his soul had gone back to God.

Sir Galahad and the Holy Grail[42]

99

At Holy Eucharist
we remember
the countless times
_____'s (name's) head
bowed at the elevation
of the chalice.

His/her last Eucharist
was viaticum,
food for the journey . . .
for he/she has drunk fully
from the Holy Grail
of suffering.

CROSS

 **G** o therefore and make disciples of all nations, baptizing them in the name of the Father and of the Son and of the Holy Spirit.

Matthew 28:19

They are happy
who
putting all their hope in the cross
have plunged into the waters
of life. . . .

Second century author[43]

_____ (name) was christened
in the sign of the cross,
and confirmed with this sign of faith.

101

May he/she encounter the risen Lord
who unlocks every tomb
with the key of His holy cross.

FLAG

y kingship is not of this world. . . .

John 18:36

Flag of the brave! thy folds shall fly,
The sign of hope and triumph high!

Joseph Rodman Drake, "The American Flag"[44]

Stars and stripes called _____ (name)
to service and to sacrifice.

> **Today, it lies quietly,**
> **at rest over his/her remains.**

As a snowquilt covers a valley,
Old Glory's spread upon our grief.

> **We pray that _____ (name) reach the full glory**
> **that only Christ can give.**

INCENSE

nd when he had taken the scroll, the four living creatures and the twenty-four elders fell down before the lamb, each holding a harp, and with golden bowls full of incense, which are the prayers of the saints. . . .

Revelation 5:8

From the altar, bathed in moonlight,
The smoke rose straight in the quiet night.

Amy Lowell, "Before the Altar"[45]

Three wise men brought
gold,
frankincense,
and myrrh.

105

    _____'s (name's) gold
was the thoughtful care
which was offered
to family and friends.

    _____'s (name's) incense
was the earthy aroma
of so many long, hard hours
of labor.

    _____'s (name's) myrrh
was the soothing balm
of compassion
and forgiveness.

(continue)

As the golden censer swirls around his/her casket, may its painful fire be tempered by the thoughtfulness showed to others, the competence of work performed, and the compassion of a lifetime. May its smoke ascend to heaven as a pleasing fragrance to our Creator.

106

PALL

et your loins be girded and your lamps burning, and be like men who are waiting for their master to come home from the marriage feast, so that they may open to him at once when he comes and knocks.

Luke 12:35

Because I could not stop for Death—
He kindly stopped for me—
The Carriage held just Ourselves—
And Immortality.

Emily Dickenson, "Because I Could Not Stop for Death"[46]

107

For every going forth,
we dress up.
Our clothing tells where we go:
The soldier in khaki to war,
the denim-clad to work,
the team in white on the road.

      _____'s (name's) white pall
      tells of a final journey.
      May this grace-filled robe,
      first received at baptism,
      gain him/her entrance
      to heaven's banquet.

WATER

or the Lamb in the midst of the throne will be their shepherd, and he will guide them to springs of living water; and God will wipe away every tear from their eyes.

Revelation 7:17

And a tear,
which evaporated somewhere in Paraguay,
will fall as a snowflake
onto the frozen cheek of an Eskimo.

Yevgeny Yevtushenko, "On Borders"[47]

_____'s (name's) life
has been like a river
through the land—
the tumbling spring waters of youth,
the twisting current of adulthood,
and the snowy passage to the bay.

May your love's tide,
now draw him/her
into an ocean of peace.

ROSARY REFLECTIONS

> . . . *all will be well*
> *and all will be well,*
> *and every manner of thing*
> *will be well.*
>
> *Julian of Norwich*[48]

For generations, the soothing "mantra" of the Rosary has provided important consolation to bereaved families and friends at the time of death. Its calming cadence and simple appeal to Mary, the mother of Jesus, has proven to be uniquely comforting to many—an assurance that "all will be well."

Many ministers of consolation have begun to use the "Scriptural Rosary" or some form or portion of it. Some add a psalm and its response, or other scripture readings and a short talk.

One way to "speak about death" with the Rosary is to offer a short mini-reflection as an introduction to each mystery. This offers another opportunity to add a poetic dimension to the reflections of the assembly of mourners.

Following are poetic introductions to the fifteen mysteries of the Rosary. It is suggested that the glorious mysteries be used for adults who have lived a full life and walked faithfully in the path of discipleship. The joyful mysteries are best used for children. The sorrowful mysteries should be reserved for those who have suffered much or experienced untimely death.

THE GLORIOUS MYSTERIES

 or those who have lived a full life.

I. The Resurrection

Easter morn, eerie light,
women with empty hearts
shocked into joy
by hollow tomb.
He is not here! He is risen!

II. The Ascension

On Bethany's highest hill
blessing as he goes,
Jesus leaves his own
but not as orphans.
He shall send the Spirit.

III. The Coming of the Holy Spirit

It was a night like this
in a room like our own—
grieving friends around,
then unspeakable joy.
Come Holy Spirit, now as then.

IV. The Assumption

Mother Mary went to sleep
and angels took her to her son.
May she open doors for all of us;
And our departed ones
usher in.

(continue)

V. The Coronation

"Holy Mary, Mother of God,
pray for us now,
and at the hour of our death."
So often said by _____ (name),
now prayed by us for him/her.

THE JOYFUL MYSTERIES

 or children.

I. The Annunciation

Gabriel speaks of the holy womb:
"Hail full of grace, the Lord with thee!"
May the angels meet this child
and announce his/her name.
"Beloved _____ (name), the Lord's with thee."

II. The Visitation

Mary could not wait to tell Elizabeth,
"The Lord has done great things for me!"
Tonight we tell of _____'s (name's) short life,
and the great gift he/she was to us.
In his/her own brief visit.

III. The Na ivity

When all was quiet and in slumber,
the heavens shone and angels sang.
_____'s (name's) life was a star in your night,
his/her death but a flicker
before a brighter light.

IV. The Presentation

Mary kept these things,
pondering them in her heart.
And today we ponder in our hearts,
now broken and sorrowful,
our love for our beloved _____ (name).

(continue)

V. The Finding in the Temple

Long ago, a child parted from his parents:
Joseph remembers; Mary knows.
They will find _____ (name) for us,
and take him/her in
till we arrive.

THE SORROWFUL MYSTERIES

 or those who suffered much.

I. The Agony in the Garden

The path from Eden,
through Gethsemane,
the bloody sweat
of our anxiety.
Jesus mercy!

II. The Scourging at the Pillar

From pillar to post,
we are buffeted,
conformed once more
to his scourging.
Jesus mercy!

III. The Crowning with Thorns

Our foreheads christened,
we resemble Christ
in our baptizing
and in our dying.
Jesus mercy!

IV. The Carrying of the Cross

Via Dolorosa—
our way to the Father—
we carry our crosses
taken up daily.
Jesus mercy!

(continue)

V. The Crucifixion

Good Friday's sad cross
already etched with Easter light.
Christ has died,
Christ is risen.
Jesus mercy!

LIST OF REFERENCES

1. Samuel Taylor Coleridge, "The Rime of the Ancient Mariner," lines 288–295, *The Norton Anthology of Poetry, Revised,* W.W. Norton Co., 500 Fifth Ave., New York, N.Y. 10100, 1975, p. 619.

2. William Shakespeare, *Romeo and Juliet,* III. ii., Washington Square Press, Division of Pocket Books, 1230 Ave. of Americas, New York, N.Y. 10020, 1959.

3. Anthony De Mello, *The Song of the Bird,* Image-Doubleday, Division of Doubleday, Garden City, N.Y., 1984, p. 24.

4. Julian of Norwich, *Meditations with Julian of Norwich,* by Brendan Doyle, Bear and Company, P.O. Drawer 2860, Santa Fe, N.M. 87601, 1983, p. 99.

5. William Shakespeare, *Romeo and Juliet,* I. v.

6. William Wordsworth, "Three Years She Grew," *Wordsworth: Poems,* Selected by W. E. Williams, Penguin Books, Viking Penguin, 40 W. 23rd St., New York, N.Y. 10010, 1987, p. 24.

7. Oscar Wilde, "Le Jardin des Tuileries," *Joyce Kilmer's Anthology of Catholic Poets,* Liveright, N.Y., 1937, p. 354.

8. William Blake, "Nurse's Song," *The Family Book of Best Loved Poems,* David L. George, ed., Doubleday, Garden City, N.Y., 1952, p. 177.

9. William W. Longfellow, "My Lost Youth," *The Family Book of Best Loved Poems,* David L. George, ed., p. 145, lines 8–9.

10. Phyllis McGinley, "What Every Woman Knows" *Times Three, Selected Verse from Three Decades,* Viking Press, 625 Madison Ave., New York, N.Y., 1960, p. 200.

11. Vincent Dwyer, O.C.S.O., *Lift Your Sails,* Doubleday, New York, N.Y. 1960, p. 20.

12. William Shakespeare, *The Two Gentlemen from Verona,* III. ii. A Shakespeare Treasury, Cotman House, Jarrold & Sons, Ltd., Norwich, England, p. 16.

13. *Romeo and Juliet,* III. ii.

14. William Shakespeare, Sonnet XVIII, *The Sonnets of William Shakespeare,* Cotman House, Jarrold & Sons, Ltd., Norwich, England.

15. Paul Horgan, *The Devil in the Desert,* Longmans Green & Co., 55 Fifth Ave., New York, N.Y., 1952, p. 58.

16. Marianne Moore, "By Disposition of Angels," *The Complete Poems of Marianne Moore,* Macmillan Co., The Viking Press, New York, N.Y., 1967, p. 142.

17. Elizabeth Barrett Browning, "Sonnets from the Portuguese": Sonnet 43, lines 10–13, *Norton Anthology,* p. 728.

18. Monks of the Weston Priory, "Wherever You Go," Recording, Monks of the Weston Priory, Weston Priory, Weston, Vt. 05161, 1972.

19. Carl Hammerschlaug, M.D., *The Dancing Healers,* Harper & Row, 10 E. 53rd St., New York, N.Y. 10022, 1988, p. 84.

20. The Desiderata.

21. Dag Hammarskjöld, *Markings,* translated by Leif Sjoberg and W. H. Auden, first American edition, Knopf Co., New York, N.Y., 1964, p. 89.

22. *Time,* October 10, 1988, p. 49.

23. William Cowper, "Light Shining Out of Darkness," lines 13–16, *Norton Anthology,* p. 528.

24. John McCrae, "In Flanders Fields," *The Standard Book of British and Ameican Verse Selected by Nella Braddy, A.B.,* Preface by Christopher Morley, Garden City Publishing Co., Garden City, N.Y., 1932, p. 690.

25. Paula Ripple, *Growing Strong in Broken Places,* Ave Maria Press, Notre Dame, Ind. 46556, p. 154.

26. Saint Augustine.

27. "The Canticle of Brother Sun, As Paraphrasd in *The Catholic Worker,*" *The Francis Book* compiled by Roy M. Gasnick, OFM, Macmillan Co., 866 Third Ave., New York, N.Y. 10022, p. 108.

28. May Sarton, "The Beautiful Pauses," *A Private Mythology—New Poems by May Sarton,* W. W. Norton Co., New York, N.Y., 1966, p. 13.

29. Samuel Taylor Coleridge, "Rime of the Ancient Mariner," lines 288–291, *Norton Anthology,* p. 619.

30. Meister Eckhart, *Meditations with Meister Eckhart,* by Matthew Fox Bear and Company, 1982, p. 49.

31. Anne Sexton, "Rowing," *The Awful Rowing Toward God,* Houghton Mifflin Co., Boston, 1975, p. 2, lines 30–35.

32. Black Elk, *Black Elk Speaks, Being the Life Story of a Holy Man of the Oglala Sioux as Told Through John G. Neihardt,* Univ. of Nebraska Press, Lincoln, Neb., 1961, p. 278.

33. Joseph Mary Plunkett, "I See His Blood upon the Rose," *Masterpieces of Religious Verse,* Edited by Jas. Dalton Morrison, Harper and Row, Publishers, New York and Evanston, with permission of Talbot Press, Ltd., Dublin, Ireland, 1948, p. 201.

34. Traditional Gaelic poem.

35. Desmond Egan, "Requiem," *Collected Poems,* Goldsmith Press, Overseas Edition, University of Maine, 1984, p. 77.

36. Eugene McCarthy, "Courage at Sixty," *Ground Fog and Night, Poems by Eugene McCarthy,* Harcourt Brace Jovanovich, 757 Third Ave., New York, N.Y. 10017, 1979, p. 55.

37. Serenity Prayer.

38. Willa Cather, *Death Comes to the Archbishop,* Vintage Books, Division of Random House, New York, N.Y. 1971, p. 50.

39. C. S. Lewis, *The Last Battle—Book 7 in the Chronicles of Narnia,* Collier, Division of Macmillan, 866 Third Ave., New York, N.Y. 10022, 1970, p. 184.

40. Anthony De Mello, p. 47.

41. Macrina Wiederkehr, *A Tree Full of Angels,* Harper and Row, 10 E. 53rd St., New York, N.Y. 10022, p. 56.

42. "Sir Galahad and the Holy Grail," from *Christian Short Stories,* Edited by Mark Booth, Crossroad Publishing Co., 370 Lexington Ave., New York, N.Y. 10017, 1984, p. 30.

43. Second-century author—anonymous.

44. Joseph Rodman Drake, "The American Flag," *The Family Book of Best Loved Poems,* David L. George, ed., p. 106, line 26–27.

45. Amy Lowell, "Before the Altar," *Complete Poetical Works of Amy Lowell*, Introd. by Louis Untermeyer, Houghton Mifflin Co., Cambridge Edition, Riverside Press, Cambridge, Mass., 1955, p. 1.

46. Emily Dickenson, "Because I Could Not Stop for Death," *Norton Anthology*, lines 1–4, p. 868.

47. Yevgeny Yevtushenko, "On Borders," *Almost at the End*, translated by Antonia Bouis and Albert C. Todd, Owl Books, Henry Holt & Co., New York, N.Y., 10011, 1987, p. 41.

48. Julian of Norwich, p. 48.

121